MIKE .

THIS IS JUST TO REMIND YOU HOW BEAUTIFUL THIS AREA THAT YOU HAVE RECENTLY WORKED IN CAN BE SO THAT ONE DAY, YOU MIGHT WANT TO COME BACK AND SEE IT (AND US) AGAIN . . . .

WITH ALL BEST WISHES ON YOUR LEAVING OUR OFFICE AND GOOD LUCK TO YOU BOTH FOR THE FUTURE IN CANADA .

YOURS . Bob .

Julia

Anne .

Yvonne

Gill

Sarah .

GOOD LUCK Mike .
I'll LOOK YOU UP NEXT TIME
I'M OVER THE WATER .

Rita .

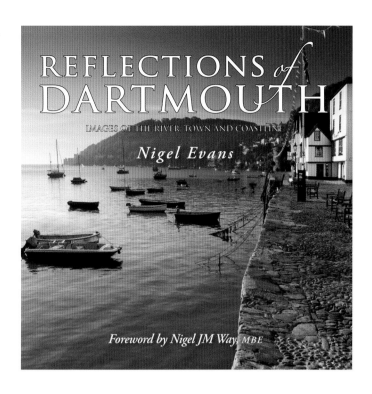

All the sparkling jewels of Dartmouth captured in one beautiful book

"A very hot and still day I remember. I stood in this spot next to Bayard's Cove Fort for sometime after taking this photograph just soaking up the atmosphere (and the heat!). One of those perfect English days that makes you glad to be alive."
so writes Nigel Evans in one of the many personal comments that caption all his outstanding photos in this book.

Some of his images shimmer with morning mists and others glitter with evening sunlight. Some were taken at dawn from the top of the nearby hills and others at dusk down by the timeless river Dart. All have made use of the special quality of light found in Dartmouth and along the nearby coast.

Dartmouth is a very special and much loved town in a magnificent setting at the mouth of the beautiful river Dart. It is also a working port, a sailing centre, the home of the Britannia Royal Naval College and a town with an astonishing history and many old and interesting buildings. Packed with pubs, restaurants, galleries and shops it is popular with visitors all the year round with the famous Dartmouth Royal Regatta being the highlight.

Along the coastline, in a designated area of outstanding natural beauty, there are some equally attractive beaches and villages.

To encompass all this in one book and retain the spirit of Dartmouth has been a challenge but Nigel Evans has accomplished it in style. Some of the most eye-catching and evocative images of Dartmouth, Kingswear, Dittisham and the South Hams coastline ever taken can be found within the pages of this lavishly illustrated book.

The three dramatic fold-out panoramas that are included display Nigel Evans' special photographic skills and enhance the impressive content of this breathtaking book even more. Historical footnotes add to the interest of this fascinating stroll round Dartmouth and journey along the coast.

A masterpiece of fine photography for everyone who loves Dartmouth and the river Dart

REFLECTIONS *of* DARTMOUTH

IMAGES OF THE RIVER, TOWN AND COASTLINE

Nigel Evans

Richard Webb

DEDICATION

Author's Dedication

To my wife Elaine, children Hannah and Tom and in the memory of my late parents Alison and Fred
Nigel Evans

Publisher's Dedication
To Gilly, my wife for her love and support and in tribute to my late parents
and the three generations of my family who have lived in Dartmouth
Richard Webb

First published in the United Kingdom in 2008 by Richard Webb, Publisher

First impression July 2008, Second impression July 2009

Photographs and text copyright © 2008 Nigel Evans
Historical footnotes © 2008 Richard Webb
Design and typography © 2008 Richard Webb, Publisher

The right of Nigel Evans to be identified as the author of this work has been asserted by him
in accordance with the Copyright, Designs and Patents Act 1988

Designed by Laurence Daeche, Anon Design Co., Christchurch, Dorset

A CIP catalogue record for this book is available from the British Library
ISBN 978-0-9536361-9-8

Typesetting: Titling: Trajan Pro Bold   Body copy: Meta Plus Book & Garamond Book Italic

• 200 pages including 6 page fold-out • 176 illustrations in colour including map
• 17,500 words including historical footnotes and Index • 12 chapters • hardback • 250mm x 250mm • 140gsm paper

Printed and bound in China Lion Production Ltd / Hanway Press Ltd

Richard Webb, Publisher
Dartmouth, Devon, England

www.dartmouthbooks.co.uk

FOREWORD

Having been invited by Richard Webb to write a Foreword to this book I panicked!

Walking back from Warfleet Creek to the Royal Castle Hotel on a freezing cold Easter Saturday I was considering what makes these images so special while I was looking down on Dartmouth and Kingswear from Above Town with the river, boats, steam train, ferries and houses tumbling from the hills - just as a child would draw a busy little port.

mists rolling in, squally showers, dimpsy evenings (my mum's word!) and moonlit nights. It's all here for you. It's taken me 25 years and I have still not seen it all!

We have all looked at some of these enchanting views but we aren't prepared to watch and wait or simply don't know how to record it to do it all justice.

We are green here too - everywhere is just a walk away or a ferry ride or a train trip...don't take the car (leave it at the park and ride).

The answer is that Dartmouth, the Dart valley and the surrounding coast are naturally very attractive and the influence of man only complements this natural beauty. I walk along the Embankment every day or walk the dog by the river to remind myself that this is the real reason why I came to Dartmouth.

The magic of Dartmouth is intensified by the natural photography of Nigel Evans - he has captured all its moods from early morning sunrise to baking hot midsummer days,

Dartmouth works its charm at all times of the day and every season of the year. I sincerely hope this book will travel far and wide and leave people with a strong desire to return to Dartmouth - or even visit for the first time.

Should I ever find myself on a desert island 'Reflections of Dartmouth' would capture those memorable moments of 25 happy years spent in Dartmouth.

Nigel J M Way, MBE
Proprietor of the Royal Castle Hotel

Bayards Cove

To Dartmouth Castle,
coast path and woodland walks
(♀ 20 MINS)

Old Market
Market days Tuesday &

HIGHER STREET

NEWCOMEN ROAD

SMITH STREET

ST
SAVIOUR'S
SQUARE

VICTORIA RD

WC

FLAV
CEN

M

FAIRFAX PLACE

THE QUAY

DUKE STREET

LOWER STREET

OXFORD STREET

HAULEY ROAD

Boat
Float

River Dart –
Sustaining life from Dartmoor
to Dartmouth

Bayards Castle
(English Heritage)
(♀ 5 MINS)

Bayards Cove

SOUTH EMBANKMENT

Lower Ferry
(car & passengers)
to Kingswear

Dartmouth
Harbour Office

Ferry to
Dartmouth Castle

BUS STOP

Passenger Ferry
to Kingswear

Book ferries from
these kiosks to
cruise the Dart

Book ferries fr
these kiosks for
Dittisham

MAP OF CENTRAL DARTMOUTH

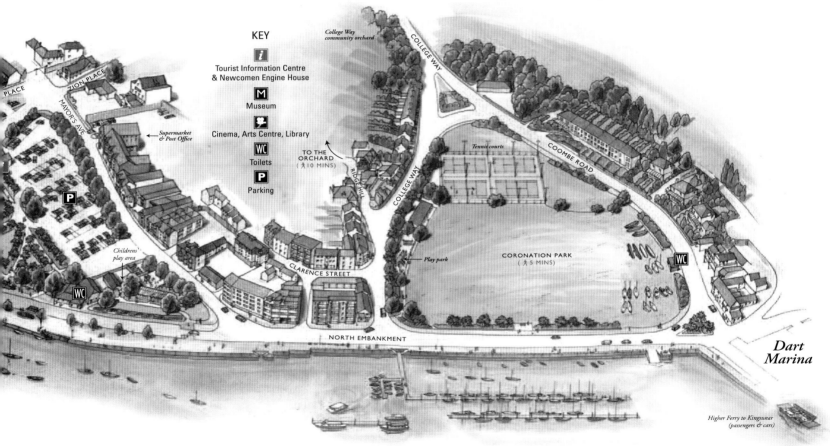

Britannia Royal Naval College

KEY

i
Tourist Information Centre
& Newcomen Engine House

M
Museum

Cinema, Arts Centre, Library

WC
Toilets

P
Parking

*College Way
community orchard*

TO THE
ORCHARD
(10 MINS)

*Supermarket
& Post Office*

RIDGE HILL

COLLEGE WAY

COLLEGE WAY

COOMBE ROAD

Tennis courts

*Childrens'
play area*

WC

CLARENCE STREET

Play park

CORONATION PARK
(5 MINS)

WC

NORTH EMBANKMENT

*Dart
Marina*

*Higher Ferry to Kingswear
(passengers & cars)*

ZION PLACE

MAYOR'S AVE

PLACE

P

P

ACKNOWLEDGMENTS

First and foremost my love and thanks must go to Elaine, my wife, without whom this book would have been impossible to produce. She has encouraged and supported my efforts over the years in spite of my attempts to ruin many a good night's sleep by getting up early to catch the dawn light. Also thanks to my wonderful children, Hannah and Tom, for occasionally admitting they quite like some of the photographs I have taken!

I must also extend my heartfelt thanks to Richard Webb, the publisher, for having the vision to produce this book and for commissioning me to create it.

Richard has published several books about Dartmouth mainly out of his great love and affection for the town and its people – Dartmouth is very lucky to have him.

Thanks also to Laurence Daeche, for his skilful and talented book design.

My grateful thanks must go to Nigel Way MBE for his Foreword. Nigel has contributed so much to Dartmouth over the years and I feel it is a great honour that he should have contributed to this book.

Finally I must thank Linda Rogers, who manages White Sails Gallery in Dartmouth so superbly for my wife and I, for her positive advice and the untiring way she has displayed and promoted my work. Without her efforts it is highly unlikely that this book would ever have been published.

Nigel Evans

HISTORICAL FOOTNOTES

All the historical footnotes were supplied by Richard Webb from information sourced from the following books and with full acknowledgment and thanks to the authors concerned (all books published by Richard Webb – see page 200 for more details):

BRITANNIA ROYAL NAVAL COLLEGE by Dr Jane Harrold and Dr Richard Porter

THE CHRONICLES OF DARTMOUTH by Don Collinson

DARTMOUTH AND ITS NEIGHBOURS by Ray Freeman

INTRODUCTION

When Richard Webb asked me if I would consider accepting a commission to create a collection of photographs for this book 'Reflections of Dartmouth' I felt very privileged and honoured. The opportunity to combine my two passions of Dartmouth and photography and have a book published is a dream come true.

I have known and loved Dartmouth for most of my life

and its unique harbour setting, surrounded by the glorious rolling South Hams hills and set on the banks of the beautiful river Dart, makes it a truly special and magical place.

Being one of the most southerly towns in the country, Dartmouth enjoys a wonderful quality of light at most times of year. This light combined with the photogenic nature of Dartmouth and its environment is what makes photography here so rewarding.

One of the area's great benefits for visitors is the ease with which it is possible (and preferable!) to travel about without using a car. There are many beautiful walks, ferry trips, pleasure cruises, steam train rides and bus excursions that all make great days out. Everywhere shown in this book can be reached in this manner.

Although Dartmouth is steeped in maritime history and contains some remarkable historical buildings it is by no means lost in the past. With some of the finest restaurants in the country, wonderful shops and galleries and world class rowing and sailing facilities, Dartmouth is embracing the 21st century with open arms. Every year a number of cruise liners and privately owned 'super yachts' visit Dartmouth further enhancing its 'Riviera' atmosphere.

However it is the locals that make Dartmouth truly buzz by organizing the annual Music, Shakespeare, Fishing and Food Festivals plus, of course, the world famous Port of Dartmouth Royal Regatta, all of which add to the colour and vibrancy of the town.

I hope this book is a little piece of Dartmouth for residents to enjoy and for visitors to take home and relive some happy times and that it will maybe inspire family and friends to visit our very special town.

Nigel Evans

CONTENTS

CHAPTER 1

BOATFLOAT AND
ROYAL AVENUE GARDENS

SUNSET REFLECTIONS

This was a very calm and peaceful late afternoon in November and the light was magical.
This small harbour in the middle of the town, called the Boatfloat, has a very calming effect
and is a unique feature of Dartmouth.

BOATFLOAT FROM
FAIRFAX PLACE

Approaching the Boatfloat from Fairfax Place, look up to your right and see these beautiful facades, caught here in the midday spring sunshine. There has been some serious distortion over the years, especially to the house on the corner, reputedly built in the 17th century. The other building here, housing the enjoyable Kendrick's restaurant, dates from 1880 and has had various uses including a newspaper office and a library. There are other houses in Fairfax Place built in the same attractive Victorian 'Tudor Style'.

An absolutely still morning in August combined with the soft early sunshine produced these wonderful reflections.

❖ *The Boatfloat was formed by reclaimed land on all sides. Ships used to moor alongside until the South Embankment was finally completed in 1885.*

BOATFLOAT PEACE

ROYAL CASTLE HOTEL

- MORNING

Here is a rare chance to see the Boatfloat and the Quay unsullied by the presence of motor vehicles. This only occurs once a year during Regatta week.

The full splendour of the Royal Castle Hotel is revealed lit by the newly risen sun which is still too low to illuminate the boats in the harbour.

❖ *The Royal Castle Hotel has its origins in two merchant houses built in 1639 before they formed the New Inn in 1736 which became the Castle Inn in 1774. It was then castellated and renamed the Castle Hotel in 1841 and finally the Royal Castle Hotel in 1902. It featured as 'The Royal George Hotel' in two Agatha Christie stories 'The Regatta Mystery' (1939) and 'Ordeal by Innocence' (1958). The ever popular 'Castle' has always been at the heart of Dartmouth's many activities and the focus of its festivities and firmly remains so under the expertise of the present proprietor Nigel Way, MBE (see the Foreword).*

Kevin Pyne, a Dartmothian and an ex-ferryman, is seen here in his role as boatman and he appears to be trying to accomplish some sort of new rope trick!

Another of Kevin's roles is that of local Poet Laureate. Much of his time is now taken up with writing his wonderful poetry mainly about his love for Dartmouth and the river. Try the Harbour Bookshop for one of his popular books (see page 200).

KEVIN PYNE

BLUE BOAT

REFLECTIONS

The water here was so still that it produced almost mirror like reflections in the Boatfloat.

This characterful old clinker built dinghy is used by Julian Distin to reach his boat which is one of the Castle Ferries.

The timber framed building on the corner of the Boatfloat is York House. This was built in 1893 to look Elizabethan in keeping with some of the other buildings in Dartmouth which are genuinely Elizabethan. Nonetheless its extravagant detailing and craftsmanship make it worthy of note. The 'chocolate and cream' building is the old railway station now used as a restaurant. Dartmouth was famous for having the only railway station in the country without any railway line. The gentle April morning sunshine and still air has produced a very tranquil scene..

❖ *The Station Café was Dartmouth's railway station from 1889 to 1972 – the only station in the country that sold tickets but had no platforms, trains or tracks!*

YORK HOUSE & STATION CAFÉ

R E F L E C T I O N S *of* D A R T M O U T H

BANDSTAND
IN AUTUMN

The Dartmouth bandstand is used throughout the year but especially during the annual Music Festival in May which has become very popular in recent years.

The bandstand itself is a lovely structure but its setting makes it even more special.

Seen here in autumn it looks graceful in the warm afternoon sunshine surrounded by golden leaves.

ROYAL AVENUE GARDENS – SPRING

The Royal Avenue Gardens are a joy at any time of year but in spring they provide a stunning show of blossoms and bulbs that herald the start of the summer season to come.

With the very mild climate enjoyed by Dartmouth even in winter these gardens are a picture. They are kept in immaculate condition by the gardeners from South Hams District Council and are a tribute to their dedication and hard work.

❖ *The Royal Avenue Gardens were first opened in honour of Queen Victoria's Golden Jubilee on 21st June 1887 and created on land that was originally reclaimed in 1671 forming an artificial island known as the New Ground, linked to the Quay (1584) by a bridge. The Bandstand was erected in 1911 replacing a wooden structure.*

These gardens in the centre of the town are an absolute gem. They have a sub-tropical feel with palms and other exotic tropical plants in conjunction with traditional English flowers and shrubs. The lush nature of these gardens highlights the wonderfully warm and mild climate enjoyed by the Dartmouth area, one of the most southerly points on the British mainland, gently wafted by the warmth of the Gulf Stream.

❖ *Corporal Theodore Veale's courage in earning a VC at the Battle of the Somme in 1916 is marked by a blue plaque and Dartmouth's War Memorial is nearby. Thomas Newcomen, Dartmouth's famous pioneering inventor of the steam-atmospheric engine in 1712 is commemorated by a granite obelisk in the gardens. An example of his invention can be found at the Tourist Information Centre nearby.*

ROYAL
AVENUE GARDENS –
SUMMER

FOUNTAIN

Here is the fountain at the entrance to Royal Avenue Gardens.

I love the way the sunlight has caught the water droplets suspended in mid air. This lovely fountain looks at its best on a bright sunny day.

❖ *The Queen Victoria fountain was presented to the town by Sir Henry Seale in 1887 to commemorate the Queen's Jubilee and was restored by the Old Dartmothian Association in 1999 to mark the Millennium.*

Just inside the Royal Avenue Gardens, near the fountain and the fine decorative wrought iron archway (designed and made by Alan Middleton, blacksmith), is this delightful and much loved small Florentine marble statue. It was kindly donated to the town in 1950 by Mr Finch Ingram, local benefactor and entrepeneur, and Richard Webb, my publisher's, grandfather.

PISCATORIE STATUE

CHAPTER 2

CENTRAL DARTMOUTH

BUTTERWALK FROM ROYAL AVENUE GARDENS

Probably Dartmouth's best known building – the Butterwalk is seen in the centre of this shot on an April afternoon.
The soft sunlight glinting off the façade reveals the wonderful detail of this 17th century structure.
The nearest end of the building was badly damaged by a German bomb in World War II but was lovingly restored to its former glory.

❖ *The Butterwalk was completed in 1640 and King Charles II was entertained there in 1671 by Dartmouth Corporation. Duke Street is named after Prince William, Duke of Clarence who visited Dartmouth in 1828. Duke Street and the Butterwalk were seriously damaged by an air raid on 13th February 1943 during World War II. After Dartmouth Council decided to demolish the Butterwalk, the Government stepped in and saved it by making it a listed building in 1945. The excellent Dartmouth Museum is located here and should not be missed.*

BROWN'S HILL STEPS

Brown's Hill Steps are typical of the many stepped thoroughfares in Dartmouth but are particularly pretty with their wonderful floral displays which the residents create each summer.

HARBOUR AND TOWN
FROM MOUNT BOONE

*This was a lovely afternoon in October
with the trees just starting to turn
golden and the gaps in the cloud
cover making for some spectacular
lighting effects.*

*St Saviour's church makes a fine sight
nestling in the centre of the town with
the low sun glinting on the clock face.*

❖ *The origins of St Saviour's church date back
to its predecessor St Clare's Chapel (1230) and
its consecration as the Holy Trinity church on
13th October 1372. The Chancel was funded
by John Hawley and completed in 1402. By
1430 it was known as St Saviour's when the
first tower clock was installed. It features in
'England's Thousand Best Churches' by Simon
Jenkins for its historic interest and beauty.*

FOSS STREET - SUMMER

A short walk from the foot of Brown's Hill Steps is Foss Street, seen here in the scorching midday summer sun.

Foss Street is a lovely place to browse the shops and galleries or stop for a coffee in peaceful surroundings.

❖ *Foss Street was originally built in 1243 as a dam with a water wheel across the creek off the river that reached up as far as the present day Bowling Green in Victoria Road. The Foss became a short cut from Hardness to Clifton – the two parts of the town that were separated by the Mill Pool until the latter was fully reclaimed in 1825. In 1943 it was bombed and an old Tudor house was destroyed.*

SIMON DREW GALLERY

One of the longest standing and best known galleries in Dartmouth is the Simon Drew Gallery in Foss Street. Famous for his fantastic combination of humour and design it is almost impossible to visit the gallery without being tempted into buying a gift for someone (or maybe even yourself!).

Simon's designs sell worldwide and it seems a real privilege to be able to buy something from the artist himself.

OLD MARKET

Behind Foss Street (to the west) is the Old Market, a lovely partly open market area where the twice weekly market is held on Tuesdays and Fridays. The wonderful array of stalls there including local craftsmen, artists, farmers, cheese makers etc, makes a visit to the market a very special experience.

Throughout the year other specialized markets take place including a monthly Farmers' Market, the annual Food Festival in October and a livestock market at Christmas. The market place has a number of permanent shops including a bakery, organic local produce, pet shop, gallery, cobblers, café and a jeweller.

One of Dartmouth's best known artists is John Gillo who until recently had a gallery in Foss Street. However he found that running his gallery left him with no time to paint. The market seemed the obvious answer.

Here is his stall at the end of a successful days trading in November – unfortunately he is very camera shy and is hiding behind the stall!

JOHN GILLO'S
STALL

FISH STALL

One of the most colourful sights is the fish stall owned by Mark Lobb with locally caught crabs, shellfish and fish, all wonderfully fresh and filleted while you wait.

THE WINDJAMMER

If you leave the market place by the Victoria Road entrance then almost opposite is the Windjammer pub.

As can be seen their floral display is amazing – an indication of the hospitality on offer within.

Dartmouth boasts a total of 14 public houses which seems a lot until you realize that in 1903 there were 26. Must have been interesting on a Saturday night in those days!

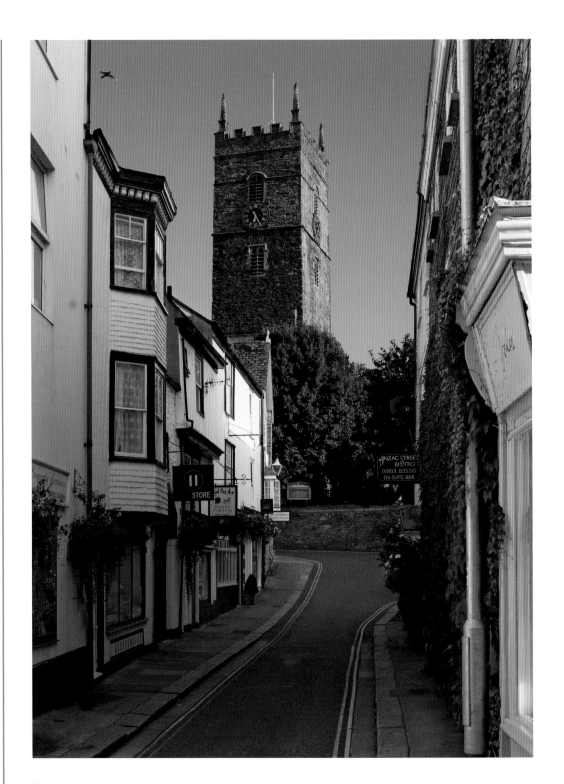

ANZAC STREET

We now head back towards the Boatfloat and directly across the road from Foss Street is Anzac Street which leads up to St. Saviour's church.

The church has a majestic air about it as it stands proudly above the centre of the town.

The shadows of the narrow street contrasts with the church tower, bathed in the warm late afternoon sun.

❖ *Anzac Street was originally called Hanover Street but renamed in World War I as German names were changed and some Australian and New Zealand troops (Anzacs) who survived Gallipoli came to Dartmouth to recuperate.*

If we go up Anzac Street, past St Saviour's church and the Seven Stars pub, Higher Street will appear in front of us. As can be seen there are some magnificent old buildings here including the oldest building in Dartmouth the famous Cherub inn seen overhanging the road in the distance. Higher Street was once the principal thoroughfare in Dartmouth because the roads below (Fairfax Place and Lower Street) were just tracks along the riverside.

HIGHER STREET

❖ *Higher Street was the main street in the town in the 14th century and at the junction with Smith Street there was a pillory and stocks. On 13th February 1943 it was bombed and a pub called the Town Arms (later demolished) was hit and two people killed.*

THE CHERUB INN

The building dates from around 1380. It was built as a warehouse and only in modern times has it become a pub and restaurant.

Taken on a late summer's morning this shot shows the way the building overhangs the surrounding streets – typical of its time.

FAIRFAX PLACE

Here we are looking from the corner of the Boatfloat down Fairfax Place towards Lower Street. The town is full of the bustle of a busy summer's day with visitors clearly enjoying the Dartmouth sunshine.

The massive bulwark of Jawbones Hill and Dyer's Wood can be seen towering over the town in the background, making the town feel very sheltered, nestling by the river.

❖ *Fairfax Place was named after General Sir Thomas Fairfax who on 20th January 1646 captured Dartmouth for Parliament from the Royalists during the Civil War. It was rebuilt in 1880 with the array of present houses with their decorated facades.*

CHAPTER 3

NORTH EMBANKMENT, DART MARINA AND BRITANNIA ROYAL NAVAL COLLEGE

DART MARINA

During 2005 the new development on the waterfront at Dart Marina was completed.

The buildings resemble traditional Devon houses but that is merely an illusion as in fact the layout of the apartments bears little relationship to their outward appearance.

This shot, taken on a beautiful July day, shows the view from the river with the clock tower of the Britannia Royal Naval College in the background.

This is a lovely sunrise scene in late August, still and tranquil with a wonderful sky.

This view looking south shows Dartmouth lit by the morning sun while Kingswear has yet to receive any direct sunlight at all. In the evening the exact opposite will happen.

The red and yellow boats on the left are the Dittisham Ferries and the pale blue boat is one of the Castle Ferries, all shortly to start a hard day's work.

MORNING LIGHT
OVER DARTMOUTH

DARTMOUTH &
BRITANNIA ROYAL
NAVAL COLLEGE

This view of Dartmouth from Southtown taken on a soft August morning shows the imposing position of Britannia Royal Naval College.

The softness of this dawn light is in stark contrast to the day which lies ahead. It is Regatta week and a hectic day of action can be expected with huge crowds and very noisy aircraft and fireworks shattering the usual peace of Dartmouth.

SUMMER'S DAY

*What attracted me here was the way
the sun has illuminated the water
under the blue boat's hull making
the water almost glow.*

*This was taken from the pontoon off
the North Embankment looking south
towards the town. Jawbones hill can
be seen on the right of the background
with Dyer's Wood on the left.*

*A lovely walk can be had along the path
on Jawbones Hill which leads down
through Dyer's Wood. The views from
Jawbones are spectacular – much more
dramatic than you might expect but it
does involve a steep climb to get there.*

Just up river from the Dart Marina and the College is Old Mill Creek seen here from the woods on the opposite side of the Dart on a spectacular April afternoon.

On the left, tied up at the quay, a number of picket boats used for training by BRNC can be seen. This quay and the pontoons are part of the College campus.

At the head of Old Mill Creek, out of sight, are a number of small boatyards. It is here that most of the ferries and pleasure cruisers from Dartmouth undergo their annual maintenance.

STORM OVER
OLD MILL CREEK

BRITANNIA ROYAL NAVAL COLLEGE FROM MOUNT BOONE

Bathed in warm afternoon autumn sunshine the College looks majestic and impressive just as intended by its architect Sir Aston Webb. He did not however design the later 'barrack' block behind the main College and was appalled when he saw it and never returned to Dartmouth again.

The College maintains strong links with the town and Dartmouth is proud of its historic association with the Royal Navy.

❖ *Britannia Royal Naval College opened on 14th September 1905. The architect was Sir Aston Webb who also designed the facades of Buckingham Palace and the Victoria & Albert Museum. Apart from thousands of Royal Navy officers it has educated two 20th century monarchs (King Edward VIII and King George VI) in addition to periods of naval training for Prince Philip, Prince Charles and Prince Andrew. Indeed it was during a Royal visit to the College on 22nd July 1939 that the young Princess Elizabeth (later Queen Elizabeth II) first met Prince Philip who was on duty to help look after the Royal Family. The Queen took the Royal Salute at the Lord High Admiral's Divisions on 10th April 2008.*

AFTERNOON DRILL

*This shot shows the College exactly as Sir Aston Webb, the architect, had intended.
He also designed Buckingham Palace and the Victoria & Albert Museum in London.*

*A new intake of Midshipmen can be seen here practicing for the Remembrance Day parade
in a few days time. They had only been at the College a week but were quickly starting
to get the hang of marching.*

BRNC CHAPEL DOORS AND INTERIOR

Originally the College chapel had solid wooden doors but to celebrate the Millennium these spectacular new glass doors were installed.

A long corridor runs the full length of the College with the chapel at one end and the dining hall at the other. The view of these doors and the chapel from the dining hall is very impressive.

The College contains a museum and many artefacts depicting the history of the Royal Navy when Britannia truly 'ruled the waves'.

Public tours of the College are run throughout the year and are highly recommended.

Bookings can be made at the Tourist Information Centre in Mayors Avenue.

OCTOBER RAINBOW

This was one of the most spectacular rainbows I have ever seen. Cynics will think that I have exaggerated its intensity but really I haven't.

Another view of Dart Marina with the hotel on the left more visible. Apart from being a delightful place to stay the Dart Marina Hotel and its Wildfire Bar and Bistro are wonderful spots to eat and drink. It enjoys stunning views over the Dart and its own marina contains some of the most opulent yachts on the river. The parasols of the outdoor dining area can just be seen on the left of the picture in front of the hotel – this has to be 'the' place in Dartmouth to eat out of doors on a sunny day.

DART MARINA,
QUAY & HOTEL

❖ *The Dart Marina and associated hotel are situated on the site of the Philip & Son Ltd shipyard that was founded in 1858 and eventually turned into the present marina and hotel complex in 1961. A floating dock was in use here from 1924 until 1961. Philip & Son built over 1500 vessels including 27 light ships, small warships, tugs, yachts and many other commercial vessels both at Sandquay and its other yard at the Noss Works across the river. The Noss Works were bombed on 18th September 1942 and twenty workers were killed and forty injured. Following Sandquay in 1961, Noss closed on 1st October 1999 ending 141 years of ship building at both these sites on the Dart..*

HIGHER FERRY

AT DAWN

At the far end of the North Embankment is the Higher Ferry, a paddle driven cable guided car ferry also known as the 'Floating Bridge'.

Here it is seen on its first run of the day on a late August morning heading for Britannia Halt which can just be made out on the far bank.

The lovely textured cobbles in the foreground are the remains of an old stone slipway long since disused but still very attractive.

❖ *The Higher Ferry, originally called the 'Floating Bridge', began operating as a steam propelled chain ferry on 19th August 1831. It was converted to horse traction by treadmill in 1836 but reverted to steam propulsion in 1867. Between 1908 and 1912 no Higher Ferry ran but it has since operated as a chain led paddle propelled ferry right up to the present day. A new larger high tech ferry will start operating in 2009, the eighth 'Floating Bridge' to cross the river at this spot.*

CHAPTER 4

SOUTH EMBANKMENT

CARDIFF CASTLE

*No visit to Dartmouth would be complete without a trip on the river. River Link operates cruises the full length
of the navigable Dart to Totnes and also trips out to sea along the coast of Start Bay and also to view the coastal wildlife.
River Link vessels sail all the year round and the boats offer full catering facilities.*

Here is Cardiff Castle, *probably the prettiest boat in the fleet, about to berth in Dartmouth
after a pleasant summer's evening cruise.*

Looking down the South Embankment with its palm trees, beautifully manicured flowerbeds and memorial benches where people fondly remember loved ones who also enjoyed Dartmouth. My favourite is probably 'Harry's' seat next to the Castle Ferry steps. Any of these benches make a lovely spot to sit and read or just absorb the atmosphere.

❖ *The South Embankment was built between 1883 and 1885 after much controversy and several law suits. In 1985 a major improvement and widening took place including raising the level to prevent flooding in the town centre.*

SOUTH EMBANKMENT

FERRY PONTOON

This was taken just at the point where North Embankment ends and South Embankment begins next to the bridge over the Boatfloat entrance.

This still, early morning shot shows the remnants of an overnight mist just hanging in the estuary. A short while later the mist was burnt off by the warmth of the rising sun. We were then treated to another glorious August day.

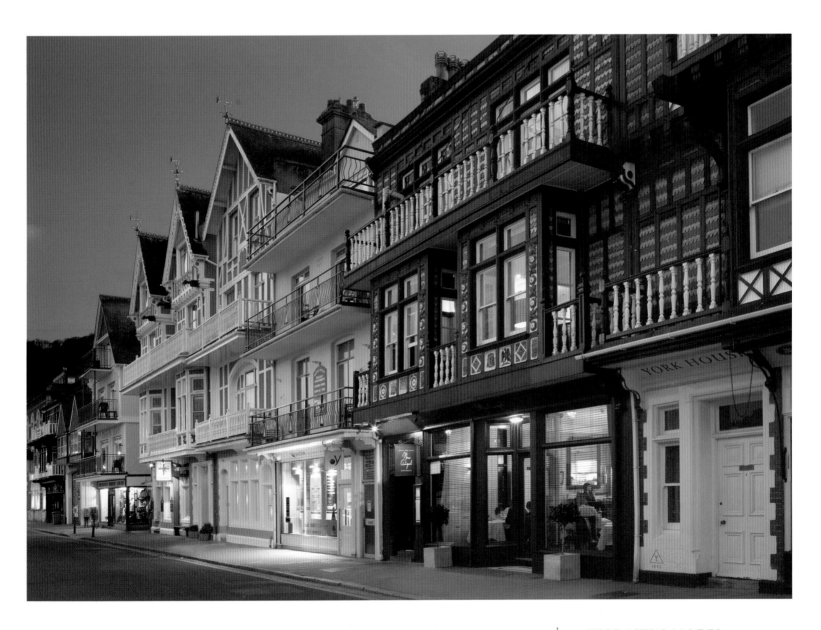

Nearly opposite the top of the ferry pontoon ramp on the corner of the Quay and South Embankment is the renowned New Angel restaurant which is a great draw for visitors to Dartmouth. Next door but one is the Seahorse restaurant, co-owned by Mitch Tonks, which specialises in local freshly caught seafood.

❖ 'The New Angel' is a famous and very popular Michelin starred restaurant which is run by celebrity chef John Burton-Race. The original restaurant here was 'The Carved Angel' which opened in July 1974 and soon became one of Britain's finest restaurants due to the skills of Joyce Molyneux, its legendary chef and co-proprietor.

THE NEW ANGEL
& SEAHORSE
RESTAURANTS

CASTLE FERRY
& OLD POST OFFICE

About half way along South Embankment is the 'Old Post Office', which is currently an estate agents, and on the opposite corner the Cottage Hospital. Also here are the steps from which the Castle Ferry operates, one of which is seen here about to depart. This was a gloriously hot summer's day with not a cloud to be seen – definitely a feel of the Mediterranean about it. Children of all ages are enjoying a spot of crabbing!

❖ *The Old Post Office would have been often visited by Flora Thompson, the author of 'Lark Rise to Candelford', as her husband John Thompson was appointed Postmaster in 1927. She lived at 126, Above Town, marked by a blue plaque, where she wrote her books. She is buried at Longcross Cemetery at Townstal, Dartmouth*

BLACK PRINCE

Fred. Olsen Cruise Lines

RED SAIL AND

'*BLACK PRINCE*'

*Another regular visitor to Dartmouth
has been the cruise ship Black Prince
from the Fred Olsen fleet.*

*I feel this shot clearly shows that,
whatever your budget or tastes, boating
on any scale is enjoyable and an escape
from the normal daily grind.*

*Relaxing on the river appeals
at every level as this photograph
clearly illustrates.*

HOT SUMMER'S DAY
– SOUTH EMBANKMENT

Another 'Mediterranean' day!

*Hot summer days in South Devon
cannot be bettered anywhere in the
world as this midday shot shows.
The Castle Ferry brings a full load
of passengers back to Dartmouth.
During the summer months up to three
boats run a constant service all day
so the next boat is never more
than ten minutes away.*

PALMS ON SOUTH
EMBANKMENT

*Just after sunrise on an April morning.
The deserted quay is a peaceful place to
take in the first of the day's sunshine.
A lovely time of year with the spring
flowers in full bloom and the trees
coming into their prime.*

CASTLE FERRY STEPS

Here is a close up shot of the Castle Ferry Achieve. The skipper is seen preparing the 'damp rag' for the next trip (a time honoured device to stop feet slipping on a wet deck)

All the Castle Ferry boats are immaculately maintained wooden vessels which are completely overhauled each winter by the skippers whose pride and joy they are.

TRAWLER
REFLECTIONS

This was a lovely peaceful spring morning and this backlit Brixham trawler, reflected in the still waters of the Dart, caught my eye.

Most of these were built in Galmpton on the Dart or in Brixham itself from where a large fleet of them used to sail out to fish in the English Channel. Steam vessels were only introduced in 1936 making Brixham one of the last fishing ports in the country to make the move from sail.

Taken from the southern end of the Embankment and looking back along its length on a peaceful August morning. The morning mist still hangs in the valley at the start of what was to be a sweltering day. The bright light and crystal clear air produced one of those mornings that really brings one to life.

❖ *The 18 pounder cannon at the far end of the South Embankment is a trophy from the Crimean War (1854-1856) and was cast at Briansk in Russia in 1826. It could have fired on Captain Chamberlayne of the Light Dragoons as he took part in the famous 'Charge of the Light Brigade' on 25th October 1854. He is buried in the graveyard at St Petrox church near Dartmouth Castle.*

CANNON –
SOUTH EMBANKMENT

EOS AT ANCHOR

One of Dartmouth's most glamorous visitors has been Eos *reputedly the world's most expensive sailing yacht costing over £100 million. She was built in Germany for an American media mogul and called in to Dartmouth on her delivery trip to America so she is newer here than when her owner took delivery of her!*

Seen here in late November 2006 the midday sun has picked out her beautiful white masts against the threatening grey of an English autumn sky. There had been a downpour about ten minutes earlier.

Eos *visited Dartmouth again in February 2008 so it seems she may become a regular visitor.*

CLIFF THE FERRYMAN

Cliff is one of the skippers on the Lower Ferry tugs. One day I jokingly pointed my camera at him and he pulled a face – here it is. Cliff is one of those people who can be relied upon to remain cheerful at all times.

If you see him on the ferry give him a wave – you are sure to get one back.

CHAPTER 5

BAYARD'S, SOUTHTOWN AND WARFLEET

FLOWERS AT BAYARD'S

This picture taken in late summer shows Bayard's Cove and the Lower Ferry Slip bathed in wonderful light early on a very bright and clear morning.

WAITING FOR THE

LOWER FERRY

As we move from the South Embankment to Bayard's Cove itself we pass the Lower Ferry slipway seen here in the morning summer sunshine.

The lone figure waiting to get to Kingswear is clearly being dazzled by the bright sunlight as he looks out for the incoming ferry.

❖ *The Lower Ferry, previously the Horse Ferry, has operated from this slip since 1846. The Marine Tavern (now Hope Cottage) was situated in the terrace on the left.*

WARM SUN AT BAYARD'S

Another shot of Bayard's Cove this time taken in the afternoon (everyone is now up and about!) with the sun behind the buildings but casting a lovely warm light onto the water in the foreground and the quay wall on the right.

The quay steps provide the ideal spot for some serious crabbing action to keep the children occupied for hours while the Dartmouth Arms, just out of sight to the right, keeps mum and dad happy!

This shot was taken from the end of the South Embankment overlooking the Lower Ferry Slip.

❖ *Bayard's Cove is from where the Pilgrim Fathers' and their two ships 'Mayflower' and 'Speedwell' set sail for America on 12th August 1620. However they then, 300 miles off Land's End, had to return to Plymouth for repairs. More recently Bayard's Cove has featured as the location for several films and television programmes including 'The Onedin Line' series.*

AGINCOURT HOUSE

We are now looking directly down the narrow street which leads to Bayard's Cove.

On the right is Agincourt House, a beautiful Elizabethan building, which is now used as a coffee house and restaurant. The lovely morning light reflected back from the houses on the quay lends an air of peace to the scene.

❖ *Agincourt House was built in the 14th century and used to have an internal courtyard. Reputed to be Dartmouth's second oldest building (after the Cherub) it was built around 1380 and then changed its name in 1415 to commemorate the Battle of Agincourt.*

Now on the quay of Bayard's Cove itself this view, with softly lit clouds and still conditions, conveys a wonderful sense of peace that a spring dawn can bring.

BAYARD'S MORNING

EARLY START

This is the first ferry of the day on a cold November morning. The only people around at this time, apart from mad photographers and ferrymen, were the newsagent and a couple of dog walkers – all of whom, except me, I suspect wished they had stayed in bed!

But for me the wonderful balance of natural and artificial light made this picture special so I was more than rewarded for my efforts. .

This was a wonderful moment when the sun bathed the cove in warmth and light while the rest of the town and river was under the shadow of a menacing cloudbank.

This effect only lasted a matter of seconds so I felt very lucky to have been all set up to capture it at exactly the right moment.

NOVEMBER MORNING

BAYARD'S DAWN

Here is another winter's morning with the first light of day just balancing the lanterns on the quay. I was especially pleased with the contrast between the warmth of the lamps on the quay and the cool light of a winter's dawn reflected in the water.

The slight blurring of the boats in the foreground and the 'soft' look of the water is a result of the six second exposure but I think this effect only adds to the gentle and relaxing feel of the shot.

LOWER FERRY FROM
BAYARD'S

A lovely fresh summer morning with the promise of a scorching day to come. Clearly taken during the 'Regatta' period with the two warships moored in the river and the cottages 'dressed overall'. For some reason the Lower Ferry seems to be full of passengers not cars – not sure why.

Taken in mid April at 6.30am this shows the benefit of getting out early. The pre sunrise light was superb with the rising sun just catching the edges of the clouds and producing a wonderfully soft warm light.

The boat in the foreground had its weathered red bottom repainted bright blue the next day which would have ruined the shot!

SPRING DAWN

BEARSCOVE CASTLE

Originally Bayard's Cove was known as Bearscove so when this 'castle' was built it was known as Bearscove Castle but it is now referred to as Bayard's Cove Fort. This view especially appealed to me because it shows the texture of the top of the quay wall and the cobbled quay surface to great effect – one of the great charms of Bayard's Cove (if a little difficult to walk on!).

❖ *Bearscove Castle or Bayard's Cove Fort is an artillery fort built by Dartmouth Corporation in 1537 to protect the harbour as part of Henry VIII's strengthening of the coastal defences. It has gun ports at ground level and a ruined stair leading to the wall walk. The fort was ideally sited to command the estuary at its narrowest point. It is now owned by English Heritage.*

SUMMER MORNING
FROM BEARSCOVE

If you walk through 'Bearscove Castle' to the furthest gunport you will find that a path leads out to a very small quay with a railing. This shot was taken here looking across to Kingswear.

At low water (as in the photograph) a small beach appears which can be seen bottom right. Also some attractive rocks are revealed which make it a great spot to sit in peace and watch the boats passing by.

KINGSWEAR FROM

BEARSCOVE

This was taken from the same spot as the last shot but in entirely different light giving another impression of the scene.

The gable ended building across the river to the left of the dinghy 'toast rack' is the Royal Dart Yacht Club which helps organize all the sailing races during Regatta week.

❖ *The Royal Dart Yacht Club was founded in June 1866 as the Dart Yacht Club and became 'Royal' in 1872. It now has over 1000 members and over 300 yachts and dinghies sail under the organization of the Joint Regatta Sailing Committee in the annual Port of Dartmouth Royal Regatta.*

STEPS TO THE SEA

Up the stone steps from where the previous two shots were taken is Southtown (the road which eventually leads out to Dartmouth Castle – via Warfleet).

Halfway up (or down!) these steps is this delightful view. I love the contrast between the cosy intimacy of the 'old town' steps and the open sea of the English Channel in the distance.

AUGUST DAWN

At the top of the steps (mentioned on the previous page) turn left and you will soon see a viewing point with seats which is where this shot was taken.

The beautiful soft pre-sunrise light was magical and proved to be the start of a glorious summer's day.

POTTERY AND WARFLEET

Continue walking along Southtown toward the sea and the views of the river to your left are superb. Eventually after about five minutes you will reach Warfleet Creek. This is a beautiful spot and you will see one of the original lime kilns opposite and the old Warfleet Pottery building – now converted into apartments. As can be seen here Warfleet is the meeting place of the beautiful South Hams countryside, the fringes of Dartmouth and the sea. The lush valley is home to many sub-tropical plants

❖ *Warfleet Pottery was originally built by Arthur H Holdsworth as a paper mill in 1819. It then became a part flour mill and part brewery in 1840 but the last Warfleet Pale Ale was brewed in 1929. The derelict brewery was taken over by Commandos as an HQ during World War II. It then reopened as Dartmouth Pottery in 1948 – employing over 200 people in the 1950s and 1960s - finally closing for re-development as apartments on 17th July 2002. Its most famous products were gurgling fish jugs!*

PEACEFUL MORNING
– WARFLEET CREEK

This is a view looking down the creek at low water on a fresh late-spring morning.

One of the lime kilns and the quay where the limestone would have been offloaded can just be seen on the right. The resultant lime produced was then taken by small boat or by cart to be used as a fertiliser by the local farmers.

Here we look back across the creek from Warfleet Quay seen on the right in the previous photograph.

The half timbered house at the head of the creek originally had a 'wet' boathouse underneath with living accommodation above. The old slipway and evidence of the doorway can still be seen. The slate and sage green house opposite is in fact recently built but has been sensitively finished to blend in with its surroundings and make the most of its wonderful situation.

❖ *Warfleet Creek (from the original Saxon name 'Welflut' meaning 'a well by a stream') had busy trading quays. The one opposite was owned by the Roope family in the 17th century and from where they traded extensively in Europe and Newfoundland. On this side of the Creek are old lime kilns. Limestone and coal was brought here by sailing barges and the limestone was then slowly burnt to produce lime which was used as fertiliser, as cement and also in lime wash for cottage walls.*

WARFLEET–
ACROSS THE CREEK

CHAPTER 6

CASTLE AND GALLANTS BOWER

GENTLE DEPARTURE

This square rigger leaving Dartmouth is so evocative of Dartmouth's history. It reminds one of how skilful the mariners of the past had been. The slightest error or misjudgement of the tides or weather could have been catastrophic.

This ship took about 15 minutes to reach the point where she would drop off her pilot onto the pilot launch which can be seen leading her out.

This is at the bottom of the steps underneath the old bridge which led out to the bathing platform.

Here is a bright and fresh new day with the morning sun bringing out the glorious autumn colours of the leaves – some floating on the crystal clear sea.

NOVEMBER MORNING –
CASTLE COVE

CASTLE COVE
– STORMY DAY

The sea here at Castle Cove is in an angry and far from peaceful mood, making a tremendous noise and smelling very briny with all the seaweed being thrown onto the beach.

My feet got very wet by the end of this session!

Here is a view from the top of the steps leading down to Castle Cove.
The autumn sunset colours and textures in the rocks combined with the peace and stillness
of the early evening made this a very special place to be.

CASTLE COVE
AUTUMN DUSK

ENTRANCE TO THE DART & DAYMARK

Once back at the top of the steps from the Cove turn left and follow the path round the back of the old fortalice wall and climb the steps up to the road. Almost immediately opposite is a gate into the woods known as Gallants Bower. Proceed up the path through the woods and eventually you will emerge out of the woodland onto the top of the hill which is the site of a Civil War fort. The views from up here are stunning and well worth the climb. There are numerous seats here to aid your recovery!

This is one of the views with which you will be rewarded. In fact there are views for 360 degrees around including back up the Dart almost as far as Dittisham.

The stone structure on the hill across the river entrance is the Daymark constructed in the days of sail to aid navigation because the hidden entrance of the Dart is almost impossible to detect from any distance offshore.

❖ *The Daymark was built by the Dart Harbour Commission in 1864, 80 ft high and 500 ft above sea level; it cost £523 at the time.*

BLUEBELLS IN
GALLANTS BOWER

From the top of Gallants Bower take the path which appears to lead down the hill back down towards Dartmouth. During May this should lead to the scene here – one of the best bluebell woods I have ever seen. This is a wonderful piece of woodland at any time of year but stunning when the bluebells and red campion are out.

❖ *Gallants Bower is the site of a well preserved earthwork fort that was built as a Royalist stronghold at the outbreak of the Civil War in 1643. It was captured by General Sir Thomas Fairfax's Parliamentary forces on 20th January 1646.*

Another view shows the bluebells and the woodland path. This is a beautiful piece of English woodland, but the glimpses of the river Dart and the sea as well, make it very special.

PATH THROUGH

BLUEBELLS

This Panorama (1)

KINGSWEAR FROM
JAWBONES HILL

This is the incredible view from the large hill behind Dartmouth known as Jawbones.

It is quite a climb to get here but your efforts are well rewarded.

This was taken late afternoon in August after a beautiful hot day.

Next Panorama (2)

DARTMOUTH
WATERFRONT

Here is the view from the Royal Dart Yacht Club pontoon on a lovely summer morning.

This image is a composite of ten separate photographs which were particularly difficult to join together because the pontoon was moving between each shot!

This Panorama (3)

MIDSUMMER'S EVENING ON SOUTH EMBANKMENT

This was taken as late as 9.00pm on Midsummer's Day with Kingswear still in lovely warm sunshine.

It was a beautiful calm and warm evening, very peaceful and relaxing.

This image is made from six separate shots, hence the apparent curve of the quay.

CASTLE FROM
STUMPY STEPS

Once you have made your way back to the Castle and visited the superb Castle Tearooms (arguably the best cream teas in Devon) for some well earned refreshment follow the signs to the Castle Ferry. You will end up at Stumpy Steps and this is the view of the Castle and St Petrox church from there.

This was taken on a beautiful morning in early spring.

Taken from the same spot as previously this shows in close up what we normally see from the town at a distance. Across the river mouth the lights of Kingswear Castle can also be seen. This is available as holiday accommodation let through the Landmark Trust. Wake up to the crashing seas!

CASTLES AT DUSK

CASTLE IN SPRING

This shot, taken from Kingswear, shows the Castle and church from yet another angle this time on a spring afternoon.

If you take one of the boat trips which venture out into Start Bay (which is highly recommended) this is the view of Dartmouth Castle and St. Petrox church that you will see. The Castle, owned and run by English Heritage, is well worth a visit with original cannons on display some of which are fired at various events during the year. Here we see the harbour entrance on a spectacular summer's day when the light and heat felt more like the Mediterranean rather than England.

❖ *Dartmouth Castle began as 'Hawley's Fortalice' built by John Hawley in 1388 and was later developed and strengthened by 1495. The Battery housing artillery facing the sea was built in 1545 and rebuilt in 1861. It was re-armed in 1940 for use in World War II. St Petrox church alongside the Castle was built in 1641 to replace a much older chapel that was recorded as originally being on the same site in 1192.*

HARBOUR ENTRANCE
FROM THE SEA

CASTLE, CHURCH
AND FERRY

A stunning summer's day! One of the three Castle Ferries can be seen departing for Dartmouth. On days like this the ferry will be very busy, full of passengers wanting to take what is claimed to be one of the most beautiful short boat trips in the country!

Another shot from the top of Gallants Bower. This shows the view looking down onto Kingswear Castle with the lush greens of the young foliage of spring and with bluebells framing the harbour entrance.

KINGSWEAR CASTLE
IN SPRING

❖ *Kingswear Castle was first mentioned in 1491 and the main construction took place between 1501 and 1503. It was restored in 1855 by Charles Seale Hayne. In 1942 a torpedo-launching station was sited nearby. It is now owned by the Landmark Trust and is available as a holiday retreat.*

MERMAID

When standing on Stumpy Steps, waiting for the next Castle Ferry, look up river towards Dartmouth and nearby on the left bank a mermaid named Miranda can be seen. Usually in the shadows under the trees she is easily missed. But one November morning my persistence paid off and I was rewarded with this glowing autumnal sunlight which for a few seconds lit her up before she disappeared back into the shadows. If you take the Castle Ferry ask the ferryman to point her out..

❖ *'Miranda' the mermaid was commissioned by Heather Robinson from the Brixham sculptress Elisabeth Hadley. It was cast in bronze by Alchemy Studio, Totnes and was installed by Brian Woodgate, the Dittisham builder in 2006. 'Miranda' is named after the mermaid in the 1948 film 'Miranda' starring Glynis Johns. Heather Robinson explains that she placed 'Miranda' on the banks of the Dart near the Castle as a visible expression of her gratitude to Dartmouth and the Dart for over fifty years of happiness that she and her family have experienced from living nearby.*

CHAPTER 7

HARBOUR ENTRANCE

'END OF THE DAY'

*This was the end of a superb summer's day in late August with the air warm and still. Whilst we do
not get classic sunsets in Dartmouth this sort of effect in some way makes up for that.*

FERRY REFLECTIONS

This is the first Lower Ferry of the day on a spring morning with just one car and one passenger. Once the first ferry has crossed the river the water never seems quite as calm for the rest of the day..

❖ *The Lower Ferry is the latest in a long line of ferries going back to the Middle Ages that have crossed the Dart at this location. It was originally a rowing boat for foot passengers and then graduated in 1840 to being a Horse Ferry rowed by two men until a steam launch took over in 1866. It closed in 1925 until taken over by Dartmouth Corporation in 1926 and then by South Hams District Council in 1974. In 2007 over half a million journeys were made on the Lower Ferry earning the Council nearly £800,000 gross.*

Another square rigger, this one resembling a frigate from Napoleonic times, leaves the Dart followed by a Castle Ferry which probably reached the Castle before the sailing ship!

The backlit sails against the dark trees on Gallants Bower must have been a sight often seen by generations of Dartmothians over the centuries.

SQUARE RIGGER
& CASTLE FERRY

SUNBURST | *Another lovely autumn sky on a huge scale, quite intimidating but also fascinating.*

What a beautiful evening. This was taken at 9pm from near the cannon on the South Embankment and diners who had finished their meals were strolling along the quay taking in the evening sunshine – memorable!

MIDSUMMER'S EVENING

PINK MORNING

Another view out to sea from Southtown, another wonderful summer dawn. It is so rewarding getting out early to experience a Dartmouth morning!

MORNING REFLECTIONS

A lovely calm and clear morning in early May. The water is in its 'pre first ferry' flat state producing these pleasant creamy reflections.

This view of the harbour entrance was taken from Jawbones Hill at dawn in early November.
It was quite cold and damp but with the mist hanging in the air and wonderful light the
discomfort was soon forgotten.

The sun had risen about ten minutes earlier right behind the Daymark but it was at this point
that the light seemed at its best because the sun is now shining down on top of the mist
in the river entrance. A few moments later and the mist was gone.

MISTY DAWN

HARBOUR ENTRANCE
– HOT DAY

*A very hot and still day I remember.
I stood in this spot next to Bayard's
Cove Fort for sometime after taking
this photograph just soaking up the
atmosphere (and the heat!).*

*One of those perfect English days that
make you glad to be alive.*

This is the classic Dartmouth sunrise shot and it really was a stunner of a dawn.

There was enough light to pick out the lovely cobbled surface of Bayard's Cove but still leave the ladders, bike and lamp in silhouette.

NOVEMBER DAWN

NOVEMBER SUNRISE

At this time of year the sun rises over the harbour mouth so about an hour later it is neatly centred over the harbour entrance which has silhouetted the Castle and church against the softly lit sky.

This shot from Bayard's Cove shows the sun reflecting beautifully on the water.

CHAPTER 8

KINGSWEAR AND RAILWAY

FOUR SAILS

*These four dinghies had just been towed to the Royal Dart Yacht Club pontoon from their berths and were awaiting their young crews.
Just behind the dinghies stands Kittery Court which must have the finest situation of any house on the Dart.*

BUSY STATION SCENE
AT KINGSWEAR

Passengers hurry towards the waiting train in anticipation of a trip back to the age of steam. This railway is the only profitable steam railway in the country if not the world. The 140 year old timber station is an original Brunel design and is still earning its keep today. Note the 'scooped' bit of the platform edge to avoid the front buffer beam of the locomotive hitting it as it negotiates the adjacent turnout (points).

❖ *The station opened in 1865 after the railway finally reached Kingswear in August 1864. It was run by the Dartmouth & Torbay Railway Co which later amalgamated with the South Devon Railway Co which in turn leased the line to the Great Western Railway Co in 1876. In 1949 British Rail took over until the line was sold to the Dart Valley Railway Co (later the Dartmouth & Torbay Railway Co) in 1972.*

This view is from the Darthaven Marina car park looking back towards the river Dart and Dartmouth. The Britannia Royal Naval College and part of the town can be seen in the background.

An excellent walk is to follow the river from the railway station to the Higher Ferry and return to Dartmouth on that ferry. After leaving the railway station turn left up the hill and this will give superb views to the left of the station, river and Dartmouth. When the road levels out a footpath leaves the road to the left over a footbridge (a good spot from which to view a departing train) and back to the line side path. This will take you over the bridge seen here and along the edge of the river to the Higher Ferry.

STEAM TRAIN PASSING

WATERHEAD CREEK

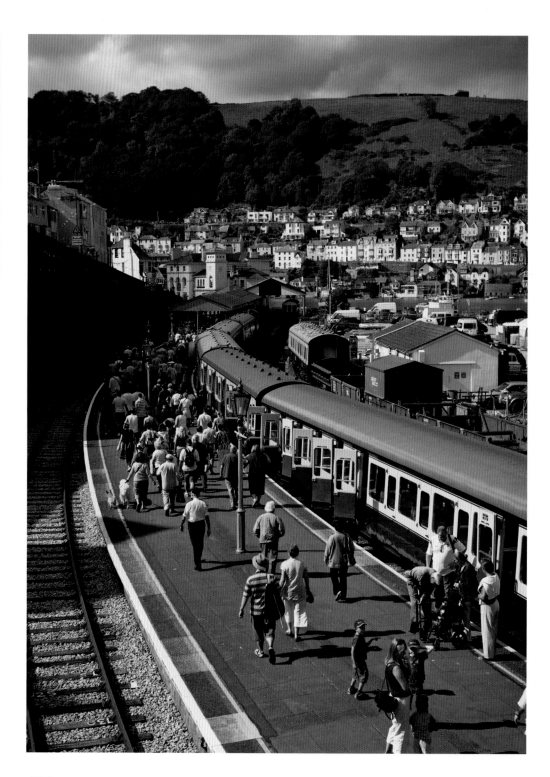

STEAM TRAIN ARRIVING

AT KINGSWEAR

Day trippers from Paignton are heading towards the passenger ferry for their short visit to Dartmouth.

In the past full length express trains from Paddington arrived at Kingswear so the station is well capable of dealing with today's flow of passengers. It must have been a wonderful feeling getting off the 'Torbay Express' at Kingswear when you had boarded it in the smoke and bustle of London.

Here is 'Goliath' approaching Britannia Halt making a majestic sight on a wonderful spring morning. These locomotives were built at Swindon and are ideal for use on the inclines of the Kingswear branch line, being both heavy and powerful. The first carriage of this train is the famous 'Devon Belle' observation car. It is well worth paying extra to travel in such style!

STEAM, POWER

& SUNSHINE

STEAM TRAIN PASSING
BRITANNIA HALT

A steam train bound for Kingswear passes the now disused Britannia Halt which is where Cadets were originally dropped off to join Britannia Royal Naval College. The main landmark here now is the level crossing at the top of the Higher Ferry slipway where you can see the cars waiting for the train to go by.

Peace and calm – a simple shot that engenders a sense of space and tranquillity.

Taken from the North Embankment mid August

MACKEREL SKY OVER
KINGSWEAR

EXCEL AT KINGSWEAR

Taken at dusk on a beautiful evening in early November as Excel berthed at Kingswear fish dock.

She had left her berth in the dark at 5.00am that morning (as she does five days a week). Her crew had lifted in excess of 750 crab pots in the day and thirteen hours later they are still hard at work unloading and preparing the boat for the next morning.

❖ *Crabbers from Dartmouth and Kingswear represent the largest crabbing fleet in the country and in addition to the local and UK market, live shellfish are exported to France and Spain on a daily basis.*

'SPINNAKER' OFF RDYC

*The sight of this full spinnaker
in the harbour with the full strength
of the August sun shining through,
with that magical sparkle on the
water, was breathtaking.*

*Very few yachts fly a spinnaker
in the harbour itself so it was
a rare treat to see one.*

LOWER FERRY
- KINGSWEAR

Here the Lower Ferry lands at Kingswear from Dartmouth. The passenger ferry from Dartmouth can just be seen berthing on the left.

This was taken at around noon on a hot summer's day with the terrace behind the Lower Ferry lit by the sunshine reflected from the wall of the opposite.

This was a gorgeous August day and Dartmouth was very busy. Here is the ideal way to enjoy the sweltering weather and get away from hustle and bustle of the town. Take the ten minute ferry ride to Dartmouth Castle and take in the relative peace of Castle Cove, Castle Tearooms and the Castle itself. If you have the energy there are numerous walks in the area (see the chapter on the Castle and Gallants Bower).

This skipper is clearly very experienced as he appears to be looking sternwards when the photograph was taken!

CASTLE FERRY PASSING

KITTERY COURT

OCTOBER DAWN

This was a cold October morning. The 'season of mists and mellow fruitfulness' was living up to its name with a beautiful warm glow of a sunrise trying to cut through the mists over Kingswear and the Dart.

This was taken from a very dewy Jawbones Hill..

EXCEL OFF LOADING

AT KINGSWEAR

This colourful scene is the result of a hard day's work for the crew of Excel *seen here off-loading the last of the day's catch of crabs.*

The catch had been sorted at sea with the premium quality crabs off-loaded first onto a refrigerated van which drove with all haste to London's top restaurants to be served later that evening (and at great expense I have no doubt!).

CHAPTER 9

RIVER TO DITTISHAM

DART EXPLORER

We start our journey up river to Dittisham with this view of the Dart Explorer passing the mouth of Old Mill Creek.
Taken on a beautiful autumn day the leaves have started to turn golden but the sky still has quite a summery feel.

ANCHORSTONE
IN AUTUMN
– HIGH WATER

As you approach Dittisham by boat from Dartmouth the river narrows considerably and also becomes very deep. At this point the Anchorstone rocks narrow the channel still further. At high water all that can be seen of the Anchorstone is a red can marker. This photograph, taken at near high water, shows the wonderful wooded banks of the Dart at this point with Dittisham in the background.

❖ *The Anchorstone rocks would have been seen by Sir Walter Raleigh and his half-brother Sir Humphrey Gilbert when as boys they learned to sail in these waters in the 16th century before going on to respectively found the colonies of Virginia and Newfoundland. John Davis a friend and contemporary, who was born at Sandridge nearby, discovered the Falkland Islands and searched for the North West Passage.*

Seen here on a beautiful day in July is one of the two boats which run a regular ferry service between Dartmouth and Dittisham all year round. This must be one of the most delightful half hour trips one can imagine ending at one of the prettiest villages in Devon. The 'boathouse' seen here is actually not what it seems – it is a tidal swimming pool on the lower floor and a very comfortable summerhouse with a balcony on the upper floor.

DITTISHAM FERRY
PASSING GREENWAY
BOATHOUSE

❖ *Greenway Boathouse was the setting for two of Agatha Christie's murder mysteries 'Ordeal by Innocence' (1958) and 'Dead Man's Folly' (1956) in which Poirot finds a body in the boathouse. Greenway House is a late 18th century Georgian house which was Agatha Christie's Devon home which she enjoyed from 1938 until her death in 1976. It is now owned and maintained by the National Trust and will be open to the public in 2009.*

ANCHORSTONE

This is another view of the Anchorstone, taken in high summer, which shows more of the rock exposed. Local legend relates that in the past wives in the village of Dittisham who nagged too much were put on the Anchorstone for one tide in an attempt to persuade them to become more mellow with their menfolk!

*This cottage, is reputedly one of the oldest on the river Dart.
It is certainly one of the most charming.*

*This photograph shows the beautiful early afternoon summer light revealing the wonderful
textures and colours in the trees of Binghay Woods and the foreshore.*

SMUGGLER'S COTTAGE -

DITTISHAM

GREENWAY QUAY

On the opposite bank from the previous shot is Greenway Quay overlooked by Greenway Cottage. The eastern riverbank at this point forms part of the Greenway Estate, with Greenway House being the home of the late Dame Agatha Christie.

Glimpses of Greenway House can be seen through the trees from the river just seaward of Greenway Quay.

This shot, taken in spring, shows the ferry from Dartmouth dropping off passengers for a visit to Greenway House, now owned by the National Trust. Well worth a visit.

AUTUMN AFTERNOON
– DITTISHAM MILL
CREEK

A late autumn view of the creek behind Dittisham which used to have a water powered mill at its head – hence its name.

This shot, looking out towards the main river, appealed to me because of the lovely way the wet mud and stones have reflected the soft tones of the sky. The yachts sitting in the soft mud await the rising tide.

148

Here is Dittisham on a very warm summer's day showing the jetty built for larger steamers to berth at all states of the tide – sadly no longer used. On the left children (of all ages!) can be seen crabbing from the pontoon where their parents can keep a wary eye on them from the superb Ferry Boat Inn, Dittisham (the pink building on the left hand end of the quay).

Behind the quay the village street rises up a steep hill towards the other village pub the Red Lion. In the background glimpses of the last remaining orchards of the famous Dittisham plums can be seen.

DITTISHAM
ON THE DART

AUTUMN LOW TIDE
- DITTISHAM

This late afternoon shot of the view from the Ham foreshore shows what lovely light this time of year can produce. The setting sun has illuminated the clouds which in turn have reflected in the water and wet mud of the foreshore.

Walks around Dittisham are a delight at any time of year which combined with a ferry trip from Dartmouth and lunch at one of the popular pubs or at the Anchorstone Café make a great day out.

FERRYMEN

Crossing the river from Dittisham to Greenway Quay is a passenger ferry which runs all year round. This is a very useful connection for anyone wishing to visit both Dittisham and Greenway House in one trip.

Here we see the ferrymen from both Dartmouth-Dittisham and Dittisham-Greenway Quay ferries exchanging notes - perhaps they have both just had the same awkward passenger!

CHAPTER 10

COAST TO START POINT

VIEW FROM ROAD NEAR STOKE FLEMING

This early morning shot in late May gives an indication of the beauty of the coastline close to Dartmouth. The way the lush green vegetation continues right up to the waters edge is remarkable and shows what a wonderful climate we enjoy.

This photograph captures the gorgeous light and freshness of spring combined with a sense of space and peace which is so special in Start Bay.

The beautiful village of Stoke Fleming is only two miles out of Dartmouth along the coast road. Here is the heart of the village and the popular Green Dragon and the 13th century St Peter's church can be found just up the hill behind me. The pub serves excellent food and is a great place from which to base a walk. The South West Coastal Path passes close by offering wonderful views of Start Bay, Slapton Sands and Start Point.

STOKE FLEMING -

SPRING DAY

AUTUMN SURF
AT BLACKPOOL SANDS

Blackpool Sands is one of most picturesque beaches in the country. It is privately owned by the Newman family and kept in an immaculate state.

The facilities here are superb. They include a café/restaurant, beach shop, canoe hire, showers and loos all of which are of a very high standard and do not detract from the beauty and seclusion of the beach. The Venus Café serves locally sourced food and drink and is used regularly by the locals out of season – which speaks for itself.

This shot, taken just after a lovely breakfast on a bright fresh November morning, gives an idea of the year round appeal of the beach.

❖ *Blackpool Sands was the site of the Battle of Blackpool in 1404 when a large Breton invasion, intent on taking Dartmouth, was defeated by a local militia under the leadership of John Hawley, Dartmouth's famous mayor, MP, privateer and merchant. Again in 1944 soldiers were at Blackpool Sands, this time the US army practising beach assaults ahead of the D-Day invasion of Normandy. The Newman family have owned the estate since 1797.*

Blackpool Sands is so called because of the 'black pool' fed by this stream which flows into the sea at its southern end. This stream and pool are ideal for small children to play in being both shallow and salt free.

This shot, taken on a spring afternoon, shows the stream in full flow. The course the stream carves out of the sand seems to change with the seasons and amount of rainfall.

BLACKPOOL SANDS STREAM

WINDBREAKS AT
BLACKPOOL SANDS

Here is Blackpool Sands in full summer – beautiful light and calm sea with brightly coloured windbreaks and parasols. Being steep the beach is ideal for canoeing and swimming (though not for surfing!).

In the season it can get quite crowded on hot days but becomes a great place for a beach barbeque on a warm evening.

STRETE GATE DAWN

Further along the coast the road climbs up above the shore affording some wonderful views across Start Bay. It then drops quite steeply back to the sea at Slapton Sands.

Where the road joins the sands is known as 'Strete Gate'. It was so named because in the past the road continued along the back of the beach to the village of Strete and at this point there was a turnpike gate where a toll was payable.

The picture shows the view here back towards Dartmouth at dawn at the end of August - bit of an early start but well worth it to see and photograph this lovely light on a deserted beach.

Behind Slapton Sands and the coast road is the very rare feature of Slapton Ley. It is a fresh water lake within yards of the sea (it is in fact very slightly salty or 'brackish' but not enough to stop many typically fresh water creatures from living there).

The area behind the Ley is a National Nature Reserve with some great walks including a boardwalk through the reed beds. This picture shows the Ley 'beach' in Torcross – the village at the southern end of Slapton Sands where the coast road turns inland from the shore.

SLAPTON LEY

DUSK OVER
SLAPTON LEY REEDBEDS

Here we see what a wonderful habitat for all sorts of wildlife Slapton Ley National Nature Reserve provides.

Many rare species including Otters, Marsh Harriers, Goldcrests, Cetti's Warblers, Ospreys and Bitterns have been spotted here.

SLAPTON LEY FROM
THE NATURE TRAIL

This was taken from the footpath which runs round the back of the Ley from the lane into Slapton village on to the boardwalk and then Deer Bridge, a highly recommended walk.

It was a lovely winter's evening with huge numbers of starlings coming in to roost in the reed beds at the back of the Ley. A wonderful spectacle.

SLAPTON LEY LOOKING
TOWARDS TORCROSS
& START POINT

This was taken from the small bridge on the lane from the War Memorial into Slapton village. The lights of Torcross village and Start Point lighthouse can be seen in the distance.

This was a very quiet and still morning and this windbreak with its vibrant colours just begged to be photographed. I particularly like the warm glow of the sunlight coming through the windbreak onto the shingle.

WINDBREAK -

TORCROSS

START BAY

AND TORCROSS

Another view of Torcross looking back towards Dartmouth from Torcross Point. This picture shows the majestic sweep of Slapton Sands which continues until the next headland in the distance.

Torcross is a great place to stop for a while with pubs, café/tearooms and a handful of shops. The views in and around the village are wonderful and include two birdwatching hides overlooking Slapton Ley and a coastal vista second to none.

❖ *Torcross village is the site of the Sherman tank memorial commemorating the loss of nearly 1000 American servicemen during 'Exercise Tiger' on 28th April 1944. Landing craft packed full of soldiers and equipment were sunk in a surprise attack by German E-boats from Cherbourg. Later on 3rd June 1944, an amphibious force of 485 ships and landing craft with US forces left the river Dart for Utah Beach, Normandy to take part in the D-Day landings.*

TORCROSS POINT

This shot looking towards Start Point from the beach at Torcross was taken in the gentle warm light soon after sunrise in August. The noise of the waves moving the shingle is so relaxing yet also strangely invigorating – wonderful!

This photograph was taken in early spring on one of those brisk and busy days when the world seems to be waking up from the long winter months. On the right of the picture the village of Beesands can just be seen at the end of the beach which connects it to Torcross.

This view from the cliff top path and shows what a great walk can be had by going one way along the beach and returning via the cliff path.

START POINT
AND BEESANDS

WINTER SUN - START POINT

The wonderful dappled light here gives this simple scene a great sense of drama and space with the craggy bulwark of Start Point and lighthouse as a focal point.

The walk out to the tip of Start Point is a splendid one with glorious views westwards to Prawle Point and east across Start Bay and, on a very clear day, across Lyme Bay.

❖ *Start Point Lighthouse was first lit on 1st July 1836, electrified on 14th October 1959 and automated on 27th January 1993. You can usually visit this working lighthouse at its dramatic location between April and September.*

SCULPTURED ROCKS
BETWEEN TORCROSS
& BEESANDS

This rather surreal scene is on the beach between Torcross and Beesands. These rocks have been sculptured by the power of the sea into these fantastic shapes.

The walk along the beach here is a hidden gem and little known by most visitors.
Going below half tide is essential to avoid getting wet, but a return route over the cliff top is well signposted so there is no danger of being cut off! This picture was taken in late May about an hour after sunrise – what a marvellous morning!

CHAPTER 11

DARTMOUTH ROYAL REGATTA

DUKE STREET DAWN

*During Regatta the whole town is 'dressed overall' and a very festive atmosphere develops. Here is Duke Street,
looking towards the Royal Avenue Gardens, decorated with bunting.*

*The sun has just risen and the low morning light is beautifully illuminating the façade of the Butterwalk.
There is very much a sense of the 'calm before the storm' as the town wakes up to one of the busiest days of the year.*

❖ *The Regattas began in 1822 but the first official regatta was held in 1834. It later became the Port of Dartmouth Royal Regatta after a visit to Dartmouth by Queen Victoria
and Prince Albert on the Royal Yacht on 11th August 1856. It is now the largest Regatta in the country after Cowes with over 300 yachts and dinghies participating.*

HMS *SOMERSET*
ENTERING THE DART

Most years the Royal Navy is kind enough to arrange for a warship to act as 'guard ship' to the Port of Dartmouth Royal Regatta. Here we see HMS Somerset, a type 23 frigate, negotiating her way into the harbour at around 6am with the newly risen sun picking out the detail of her superstructure.

The arrival of a large ship into the Dart is always preceded by a very long blast on the ship's horn to warn other traffic to keep clear. In the hours leading up to 'D-Day' in June 1944 a total of 485 ships and landing craft left the Dart – it must have been an awesome sight!

'CAFÉ ALF RESCO'
IN REGATTA MOOD

Café Alf Resco does everything with great enthusiasm and Regatta is no exception as you can see! For many visitors and locals alike a hearty 'Alf's' breakfast sets them up for a full day of Regatta fun - especially if they are taking part in any of the many energetic activities afloat or ashore for which Dartmouth's Regatta has become famous.

HEADING OUT
TO RACE

Each Regatta morning the enormous fleet of racing yachts leave their overnight berths and head out to race in Start Bay. This was a beautiful August day with the weather looking perfect for a good day's racing.

This view taken from Above Town shows the start of the exodus.

There are a number of clues which reveal this as a Regatta shot.

The warship in the background dressed overall with bunting, then the public address caravan on the corner of the Boatfloat in the middle distance. In the Boatfloat two whalers await the waterborne Tug O' War, on the ground are the remains of the children's pavement painting competition and the deck chairs remain from the previous evening's Firework Spectacular.

The clear morning light renders a splash of quiet beauty in the bustle of the Regatta.

REGATTA MORNING

WHALER RACING

Most of the local pubs and cafés enter teams into the whaler racing competitions using a mixture of staff and regulars to make up the crews. This racing is taken very seriously in the town with many crews putting in regular practice in the preceding months.

Both the car and passenger ferries to Kingswear can be seen in the background and they have to steer a very careful path through all the racing.

This was a lovely morning with the sunshine fighting its way through the patchy mist to create a wonderfully soft, almost surreal, light. The idea that warships could be seen as romantic and beautiful seems unlikely – perhaps only at Dartmouth Regatta could such a thing happen?

REGATTA MIST

FRIGATE REFLECTIONS

Another gorgeous sunrise showing power and beauty!

RED ARROWS

OVER THE RIVER DART

For many the highlight of Regatta is the display by the Red Arrows. The contours of the Dart estuary make their display far more dramatic here than at any other venue.

This picture taken from Jawbones hill shows the team of nine doing their best to impress their colleagues in the Royal Navy below!

RED ARROWS OVER
RIVER DART ENTRANCE

*What can one say? The Red Arrows over
Dartmouth harbour entrance on a fine
Regatta evening – breathtaking!*

DUSK FIREWORKS

Even at the end of August at 9pm it is sometimes not fully dark – this is just such an occasion. Here we see one of the first bursts of the evening being watched by the passengers of a cruise ship which has delayed its departure so that they can see the display.

*A similar shot taken near the end of the display by which time it was almost fully dark.
The firework displays are amongst the finest to be seen anywhere and normally take place
on the Thursday and Saturday evenings of the Regatta at 9pm.*

REGATTA FIREWORKS

REGATTA EVENING
- BOATFLOAT

The happy crowd spills onto the road from the Royal Castle Hotel in contrast to the calm and tranquil Boatfloat. This scene sums up Dartmouth Regatta – good natured festive fun combined with the charm and underlying tranquil nature of the river and town.

CHAPTER 12

CHRISTMAS AND NEW YEAR

FOSS STREET - CHRISTMAS

Foss Street is a wonderful place to shop and is full of Christmas cheer. This narrow pedestrian street creates a lovely intimate atmosphere especially during the festive season.

Dartmouth has a magical air at Christmas with the narrow streets festively decorated and a very convivial atmosphere in all the shops, cafés and pubs. Traders in the town make great efforts to celebrate Christmas in style and the relative peace compared with the big cities makes shopping here a very pleasurable experience.

CHRISTMAS

– ANZAC STREET

The bunting and lights over Anzac Street and Foss Street combine to form a virtual arch when viewed from near St Saviour's church. Try the Anzac Bistro, on the left, that specializes in well cooked local produce.

186

As always Café Alf Resco does things in style and Christmas is no exception.

In addition to the usual 'scrummy' offerings Alf's lay on superb seasonal extras such as pannetone and their own 'Christmas marmalade'.

CAFÉ ALF RESCO
IN CHRISTMAS MOOD

CHRISTMAS MARKET

Even the market place gets dressed up for Christmas!

Here is one of various events held in the run up to the big day in addition to the usual Tuesday and Friday market days.

FOSS STREET
AT CHRISTMAS

This photograph was taken at dusk looking towards St Saviour's church which reminds us gently of the true focus of Christmas.

The girl nearest the camera is somewhat blurred because in her enthusiasm to finish her Christmas shopping she moved quite a way in the one third of a second it took to expose this photograph!

CHRISTMAS IN
DUKE STREET

This was taken on the evening of
'Candlelit Dartmouth' when candlelit
processions starting from different
parts of the town converge on the Royal
Avenue Gardens for everyone to enjoy
the carol singing and the festive market.

The decorative lights reflected in the Boatfloat make a wonderful sight which combined with the sound of carols from the bandstand create a very 'Christmassy' atmosphere.

BOATFLOAT CHRISTMAS

ROYAL CASTLE HOTEL
AT CHRISTMAS

The threatening sky overhead is in stark contrast to the warm, festive and cosy atmosphere of a Dartmouth Christmas. The Royal Castle Hotel adds to the mood, as always, in its imaginative 'gift wrapped' guise.

CHRISTMAS
– FAIRFAX PLACE

The view down to the Boatfloat through Fairfax Place.

*White Sails Gallery and the famous Harbour Bookshop, opened in 1951 by Christopher Milne
(who was described as Christopher Robin by his father A.A. Milne in the Winnie the Pooh books)
are both prominent in this shot. This book is available from both of these establishments
so it would seem inappropriate not to include them – especially as my wife and I own
White Sails Gallery (see page 199)!*

After the indulgences of New Year's Eve a number of intrepid souls make their annual leap into the Dart. They all mumble something about raising money for charity but many believe that is just a cover and that blowing away the cobwebs of seasonal excess is the real reason!

NEW YEAR'S DAY –

BAYARD'S COVE

INDEX

DISCLAIMER

The author and publisher have made every effort to find and correctly attribute the copyright of material that is not already in the public domain but if they have inadvertently used or credited any material inappropriately, please could the copyright holder contact the author or the publisher so that a full credit can be given in the next edition.

PHOTOGRAPHER'S NOTES

All the photographs have been shot digitally using a variety of cameras from an Olympus E20P to, more recently, a Canon EOS 5D.

The majority were captured in 'Raw' mode with bracketed shots being combined to produce 'high dynamic range' final images. My aim has always been to reproduce as accurately as possible what my eyes saw at the time the photograph was created.

This usually requires some degree of post production work.

Most adjustments made have been at the 'Raw' conversion stage mainly to levels, curves, colour temperature and saturation.

www.nigelevansphotographer.com

NIGEL EVANS

Nigel Evans was born and brought up in Nottingham, about as far inland as it is possible to get in England, but his love of the sea and coast developed during early childhood holidays and sailing trips with his family off the South Devon coast. Nigel's father Fred, who had served as a naval officer during World War II, never missed an opportunity to go sailing and his passion for all things nautical had a profound effect on Nigel as a boy.

Nigel has always had a keen interest in photography after being given a 'Brownie' box camera as a small child. His interest blossomed when he discovered the school darkroom where he slowly mastered the art of developing and printing.

With no formal training Nigel has progressed from keen amateur to a semi-professional photographer over the last decade after he and his wife Elaine opened the White Sails Gallery in Dartmouth.

WHITE SAILS GALLERY

FRAMED AND CANVAS MOUNTED PRINTS

All the photographs in *Reflections of Dartmouth* (and many more) are available as signed prints, either framed or canvas mounted, at White Sails Gallery (opposite the Harbour Bookshop).

White Sails have many works by local artists as well as prints and limited editions, all framed or canvas mounted and ready to hang.

Delivery can be made anywhere in the U.K. (or indeed the world by arrangement)

Open 7 days a week all year round.   Monday – Saturday 10.00am – 5.00pm   Sunday 11.00am – 4.00 pm

1, St George's Square, Dartmouth, Devon TQ6 9AQ   Telephone/Fax 01803 832272   www.whitesailsgallery.com

BOOKS OF QUALITY AND INTEREST

Britannia Royal Naval College, Dartmouth
An Illustrated History
Dr Jane Harrold and Dr Richard Porter
- 208 pages • 323 illustrations including 118 in colour 32 in sepia and 173 in black & white
- 85,000 words • hardback • 279mm x 279mm

ISBN 978-0-9536361-7-4

Reflections of Dartmouth
Images of the River, Town and Coastline
Nigel Evans
- 200 pages including 6 page fold-out
- 176 illustrations in colour including map
- 17,500 words • hardback
- 250mm x 250mm

ISBN 978-0-9536361-9-8

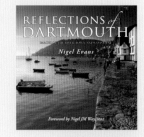

Dartmouth Ghosts & Mysteries
Tales of the Town and its Villages
Ken Taylor
- 128 pages • 32 illustrations including 5 in colour
- colour endpapers • 52,000 words • hardback
- 245mm x 165mm

ISBN 978-0-9536361-5-0

John Hawley
Merchant, Mayor and Privateer
Michael Connors
- 168 pages including 8 in colour
- 70 illustrations including 21 in colour and 5 maps
- colour endpapers • 73,000 words • hardback
- 234mm x 156mm

ISBN 978-0-9536361-8-1

Further up the River
and fifty other poems
Kevin Pyne
- 100 pages • 4 illustrations including 3 in colour
- colour endpapers • hardback
- 210mm x 150mm

ISBN 978-0-9536361-2-9

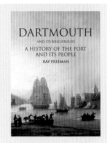

First across the Line
and fifty other poems
Kevin Pyne
- 100 pages • 4 illustrations including 3 in colour
- colour endpapers • hardback
- 210mm x 150mm

ISBN 978-0-9536361-4-3

Dartmouth and its Neighbours
A History of the Port and its People
Ray Freeman
- 224 pages • 126 illustrations including 24 maps
- colour endpapers • hardback
- 245mm x 184mm

ISBN 978-0-9536361-6-7

The Chronicles of Dartmouth
An Historical Yearly Log 1854 – 1954
Don Collinson
- 300 pages • 468 illustrations including 45 in colour • 125,000 words • hardback
- 295mm x 210mm

ISBN 978-0-9536361-0-5

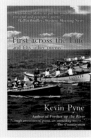

Available from **The Harbour Bookshop, Dartmouth**
The Harbour Bookshop, 12 Fairfax Place, Dartmouth, Devon TQ6 9AE   Tel & Fax: 01803 832448   Email: harbourbookshop@hotmail.co.uk

Published by Richard Webb, Dartmouth
www.dartmouthbooks.co.uk